The Learning to BREATHE

STUDENT WORKBOOK

SECOND EDITION

A Six-Week Mindfulness Program for Adolescents

PATRICIA C. BRODERICK, PHD

New Harbinger Publications, Inc.

Publisher's Note

NEW HARBINGER PUBLICATIONS is a registered trademark of New Harbinger Publications, Inc.

Distributed in Canada by Raincoast Books

All artwork appears courtesy of Jill Design Studio.

Cover design by Amy Shoup

Acquired by Catharine Meyers

Edited by Brady Kahn

Printed in the United States of America

23   22   21

10   9   8   7   6   5   4   3   2

Six-Session Student Workbook

"MINDFULNESS is paying attention in a particular way:
on purpose, in the present moment, and nonjudgmentally."

—Jon Kabat-Zinn

B   Listen to your **Body**

R   **Reflections** (thoughts) are just thoughts

E   Surf the waves of your **Emotions**

A   **Attend** to the inside and the outside

T   Try **Tenderness**—Take it as it is

H   Practice **Healthy** habits of mind

E   Gain the inner edge. Be **Empowered**!

Theme B: My Mindful/Mindless Life

What things (or activities) in your life do you do on automatic pilot (mindlessly)? What are the things you do that fully engage you (mindfully)? Fill in the boxes with as many examples as you can name. You can also write about how you feel when you do things mindfully (with attention) or mindlessly (without attention).

My Mindful Life...

_____

_____

_____

_____

_____

_____

_____

_____

My Mindless Life...

_____

_____

_____

_____

_____

_____

_____

_____

Theme B: Mindfulness in My Life

You can practice mindful attention in all of the moments of your day.

As an experiment, select an activity as "your practice": a simple daily activity that you choose to do mindfully on a regular basis. Pick one of these examples or come up with your own. Do this activity with

awareness and interest; really "be there" for this simple activity. Try adding one new practice each week.

- ○ Washing your face

- ○ Going up and down stairs

- ○ Washing dishes

- ○ Getting dressed

- ○ Getting or preparing a snack

- ○ Eating breakfast

- ○ Answering a phone call

- ○ E-mailing

- ○ Driving to a certain place

- ○ Waiting at a red light

- ○ Walking down a hallway

- ○ Eating lunch

- ○ Opening and closing your locker

- ○ Walking a pet

- ○ Washing your hands

- ○ Texting

- ○ Standing in line

- ○ Waiting for a bus

- ○ Listening to someone

- ○ Brushing your teeth

- ○ Other _____

- ○ Other _____

My Home Practice: Theme B

1. Practice mindful breathing for at least three breaths at a time, three times per day.

2. Practice the "Body Scan" with audio (which should be provided by your teacher) _____ times.

3. Try the "Three-Minute Body Scan," described next in this workbook, each day in school or in some other place.

4. Practice your own special activity mindfully (from theme B, "Mindfulness in My Life"). Note your observations and reflections in the lines below.

Observations and Reflections:

_____

_____

_____

_____

_____

_____

_____

_____

_____

_____

_____

_____

_____

_____

_____

Theme B: Tips to Take Away: Three-Minute Body Scan

You can do a short "Body Scan" at any time, especially if you notice that you're feeling tense or anxious.

Try it:

- while seated in class

- before tests

- before athletic events

- before speaking in public

- before getting out of bed in the morning

- before falling asleep

- while standing in line

- during social events

- before an interview

How to do it:

1. Use your attention to find your breath in your body.

2. Starting from either your feet or your head, move your attention through your body and notice your experience. Scan for tension in your feet; lower back; stomach; shoulders; face, jaw, or forehead; or wherever you hold tension in your body.

3. As you scan each area, breathe into the area, releasing tension and bringing in new energy as you did in the "Body Scan."

4. Expand your awareness to your entire body and feel the breath move from your head to your feet.

Theme R: Big Event Circles

Story 1

Write your thoughts in the circle below.   Write your feelings in the circle below.

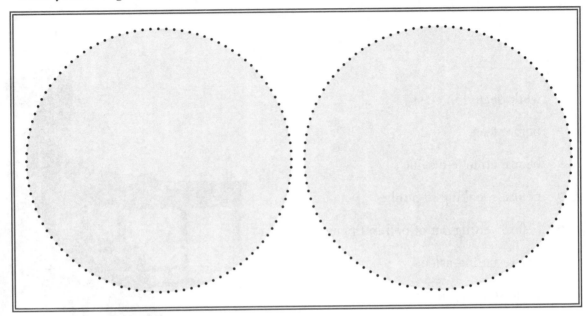

Story 2

Write your thoughts in the circle below.   Write your feelings in the circle below.

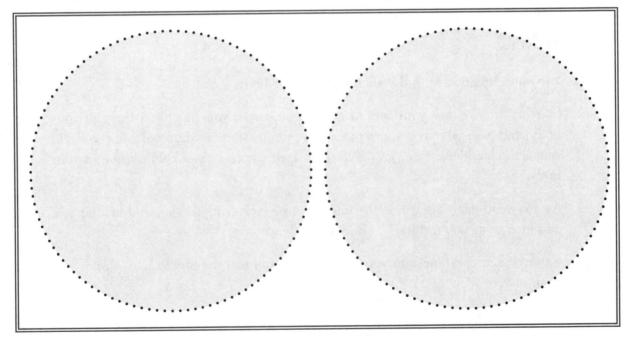

My Home Practice: Theme R

1. Practice mindful breathing for at least three breaths at a time three times per day.

2. Practice a short period of mindfulness of thoughts (once a day, ideally; use the audio that should be provided by your teacher).

3. Use the workbook activity on the next page, "Dealing with Troubling Thoughts," to help you when you practice.

4. Continue practicing mindfulness in your day-to-day life, especially in your personal-choice area (from "Mindfulness in My Life"). Note your observations and reflections in the lines below.

R

Observations and Reflections:

_____

_____

_____

_____

_____

_____

_____

_____

_____

_____

_____

_____

_____

_____

Theme R: Tips to Take Away: Dealing with Troubling Thoughts

Notice the thoughts that are arising in your mind.

Try the mindful approach:

1. Become aware of what your mind is doing: *thinking*. It's generating thoughts. The thought is like a bubble that arises in the space of the mind. It's just what the mind does.

2. Step back and examine the thought with curiosity. How loud or soft is it in your mind? How strong is it? How long does it last? Can you notice sensations in your body when the thought arises? Don't try to push it out of your mind. Just observe.

3. Get in touch with your breath as you observe the thought. Remember, it's just a thought. Don't struggle with it, because that can make it stronger.

4. Watch the thought change in intensity. Return your full attention to your breath.

My Home Practice: Theme E

1. Practice mindful breathing for at least three breaths at a time three times per day.

2. Do a short mindfulness practice on feelings (once a day, ideally; use the audio that should be provided by your teacher).

3. Begin to notice thoughts, feelings, and physical sensations as they arise throughout the day.

4. Practice being kind to yourself when uncomfortable feelings arise. Don't try to push them away. Just notice them and where they show up as sensations in your body.

5. Keep practicing mindfulness in your day-to-day life, especially in the practice of your choice (from theme B, "Mindfulness in My Life"). Note your observations and reflections in the lines below.

Observations and Reflections:

_____

_____

_____

_____

_____

_____

_____

_____

_____

_____

_____

_____

E

Theme E: Tips to Take Away: About Anger and Other Uncomfortable Emotions

Anger is an emotion that has a long list of close relatives: irritation, frustration, impatience, rage, hatred, annoyance, resentment, irritability, crankiness, and so forth. Anger and its variations can cause us to "heat up." Notice the way we refer to angry feelings, for example, "boiling mad," "hotheaded," or "seeing red." Anger impairs our thinking and can feel overwhelming. It makes us lose our balance. Sometimes when we're angry, we act impulsively in ways that end up hurting ourselves and others. Shouting, threatening, fighting, rudeness, disrespect, and name-calling are a few examples. Sometimes we take out our anger in quieter ways by gossiping and excluding others and making them feel bad. Most of all, anger can hurt our health, well-being, and social relationships. Chronic anger ramps up the stress response and reduces our own level of happiness.

Kick the anger habit!

Try a mindful approach to difficult emotions. When you feel yourself getting angry:

1. Stop and pay attention. Notice with interest where you are feeling the anger in your body. What does this experience feel like for you?

2. Turn your attention toward the feelings as they arise: Are they sharp, hard, soft, intense, fast, slow, burning? Are they moving around in your body? Are they centered in one place? Do they change as you observe them?

3. Experience the feelings of anger as waves, coming and going. Don't try to block them, avoid them, or get rid of them. Don't try to hold on to them or keep them going. Just don't act on the angry feelings right now. You can view anger as a strong energy in the body and mind, like a sudden storm.

4. Tune in to the breath and see if you can ride the waves of the anger and watch them get smaller and smaller. Be kind to yourself if this is hard to do.

Now you're in a better position to make a smart decision about how to act.

Remember: You can use this approach to work with any difficult feelings. Just substitute the name of a feeling in the steps above. Surf the waves of your annoyance, boredom, sadness, disappointment, jealousy, and so on. Breathe and watch the feelings rise and fall. They're not fun, but they will pass. And you will become more empowered.

Theme A: What's the Best Balance?

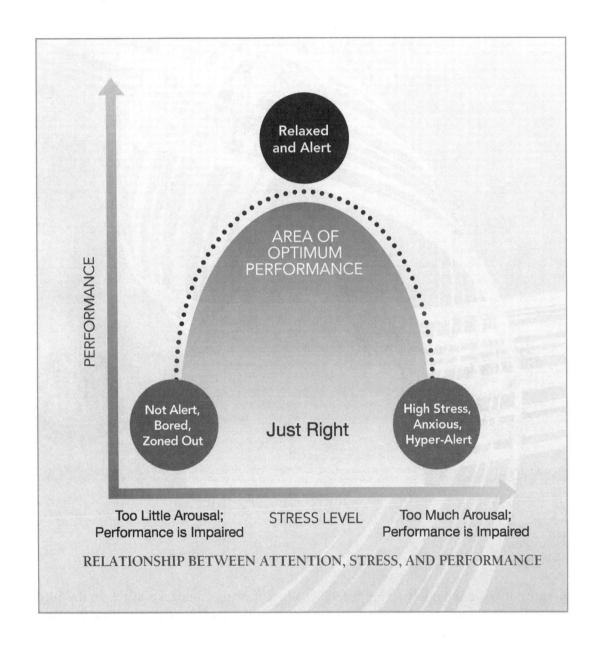

RELATIONSHIP BETWEEN ATTENTION, STRESS, AND PERFORMANCE

Theme A: What's My Limit?

SHORT TERM STRESS

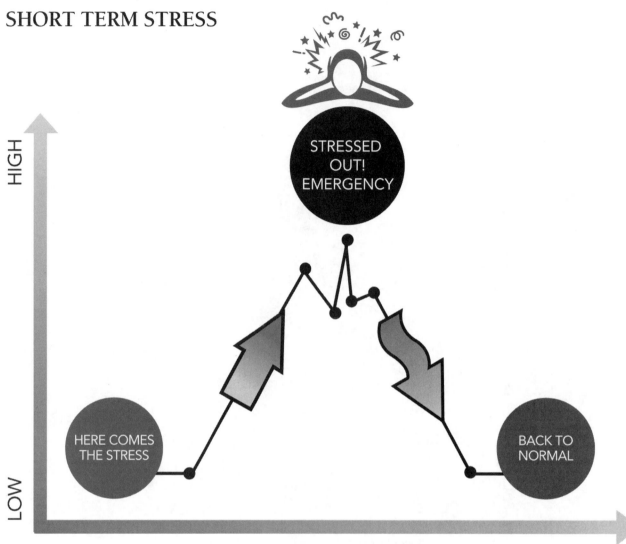

Did you know?

- You can notice your body's stress response when it occurs because of the many physical changes involved. Your heart races, your palms sweat, your breath gets more shallow, and so forth. Your body's stress response is intended to help you deal with threats.

- Some foods (cola, coffee, tea, chocolate) and drugs (nicotine) also cause a stress-like reaction in your body.

- Our bodies respond to psychological stressors in the same way that they respond to physical threats.

- Our perceptions play a major role in whether or not we feel stressed.

A

LONG TERM CHRONIC STRESS

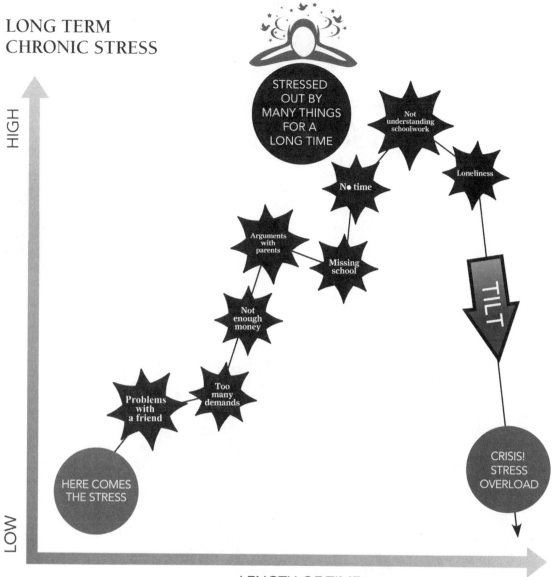

HIGH

LOW

STRESSED OUT BY MANY THINGS FOR A LONG TIME

Not understanding schoolwork

Loneliness

No time

Arguments with parents

Missing school

Not enough money

Too many demands

Problems with a friend

HERE COMES THE STRESS

TILT

CRISIS! STRESS OVERLOAD

LENGTH OF TIME

A

List your chronic stressors

1. _____
2. _____
3. _____
4. _____
5. _____

6. _____
7. _____
8. _____
9. _____
10. _____

Circle your top three stressors.

Theme A: What Happens When We Practice Mindfulness

Mindful Awareness

Increased Regulation

Prefrontal cortex

Amygdala

Decreased Reactivity

Theme A: Sitting Postures:

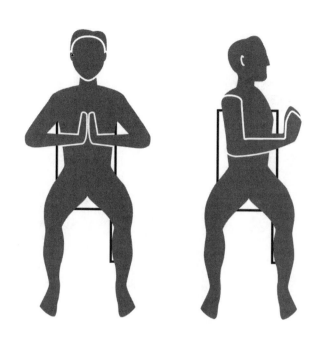

Palm Press

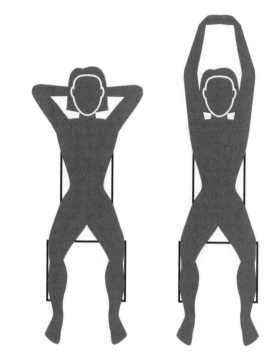

Upward Stretch

Seated Tree

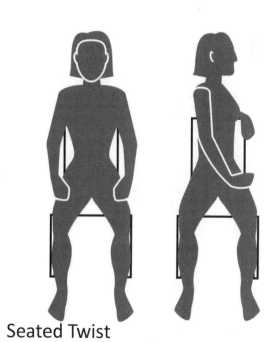

Seated Twist

A

Theme A: Standing Postures:

Mountain Pose

Upward Stretch

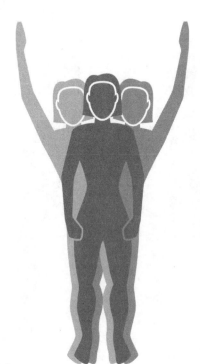

Reach Up

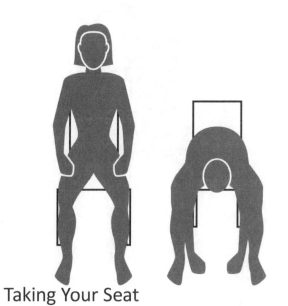

Taking Your Seat

Theme A: Memo from the Body-Mind

To: Body-Mind Owners: All Makes and Models

From: Your Stress-Response System

Re: Your Stress

Message: High Priority!

Dear Owner:

As the system primarily involved in your body-mind's stress response, we want to keep you informed about our operations so that you will be in a better position to keep us in good working order. Your body-mind's stress response came with your basic equipment. It is intended to prepare you to fight, flee, or freeze in case of a real emergency so that you can survive.

Specifically, we are a coordinated group that includes the *autonomic nervous system* (ANS) and the *hypothalamic-pituitary-adrenal axis* (HPA axis for short). Here's how we operate. You have a threat detector located deep inside your brain called the *amygdala*. When the amygdala registers the information that your safety is threatened or that there's something out there to worry about, the *sympathetic part* (SNS) of the *autonomic nervous system* (ANS) leaps into action to help protect you. Your brain immediately sends signals to the interior of the *adrenal glands*, which sit on top of your kidneys, telling them to release the hormone (and neurotransmitter) *adrenaline* into your bloodstream. Remember that hormones are chemical messengers that have powerful effects on your body-mind. If you can recall feeling your hair stand on end, your heart beginning to pound, your palms beginning to sweat, and your stomach turning (possibly when faced with a test you didn't expect), you know our power to get your system revved up to fight, freeze, or run away.

We also provide an additional homeland-security system called the HPA axis. Two of our components (*hypothalamus* and *pituitary*) are located deep in the brain. After a red alert from the amygdala, the hypothalamus gets this ball rolling by secreting hormones into the hypothalamic-pituitary circulatory system. The principal one is *CRH* (*corticotrophin-releasing hormone*), which triggers the pituitary to release *ACTH* (also called corticotrophin). ACTH jump-starts the adrenals to release another stress hormone, called *cortisol*, from their surface into the bloodstream. If you've ever been scared to death watching a horror movie alone at night, you know that adrenaline works within seconds, but cortisol backs it up over the course of minutes or hours. It takes about an hour for the effects of cortisol to leave the system. When the stressful situation is over and you have prevailed, the other arm of the ANS, called the *parasympathetic nervous system* (PNS), moves into action by relaxing your body-mind and allowing it to rebalance in preparation for the next threat. The *vagus nerve* that originates in the brain is part of the PNS and sends signals to the heart and other organs that regulate the heartbeat (among other things). The heartbeat slows down as a result of activation of the vagus nerve. It works like a brake on the stress-response system. When you inhale, you activate the sympathetic system, and when you exhale, you activate the parasympathetic system. That's why some relaxation practices teach extending the exhalation to strengthen the parasympathetic (or "cool-down") response. Let's try it. Take a deep breath right now, and then exhale through your mouth in a slow, long, smooth sigh. Whew! Thank goodness for that.

Anyway, so much for our trusty apparatus.

A

It has come to our attention that many owners are activating the stress-response system for extended periods of time without a break. Because owners might not realize the damage they do to their systems when they are under constant stress, we take the opportunity in this memo to present it in some detail.

We find it hard to believe that this constant activation is due to unceasing, real threats on owners' health and safety (such as constantly coming face-to-face with wild animals or other equally scary situations). We've been told that owners are activating their systems because of internal threats like worries, fears, anger, resentments, foiled expectations, disappointments, and so forth. Now, we acknowledge that life can be really tough. We have the greatest sympathy for what owners are going through. However, we—the elements of your stress system—need to inform you of the fact that we are being overworked when the stressful events that keep us going are happening in owners' minds. In other words, owners who constantly ruminate, let problems fester, hold on to jealousy, or continually feed the fires of anger are really wearing us out!

Here's the view from the inside. Constant activation of the system results in too much cortisol pumping into the bloodstream. Too much cortisol dismantles your *immune system*. Remember the immune system? Immune system cells are constantly on patrol, killing invaders and saving you from illness. Without a well-functioning army of immune cells, your body isn't going to heal from invaders very well. If you get sick (low immunity) during exam time (high stress), don't say we didn't warn you.

Too much cortisol also damages and even kills cells in your brain (*hippocampus*) that are responsible for learning and memory. That's not going to help you graduate! Stress hormones like adrenaline cause the heart to pump blood faster, potentially resulting in high blood pressure and damage to your arteries because of the force of blood on the delicate vessels. Stress hormones like cortisol increase your appetite, especially for comfort food, because your body reads their chemical message as "Yikes! An emergency! Better store up some energy so I can run away when I need to." Stress hormones are related to stomach discomfort, and you know that's no fun either. Recall that it takes about an hour for the body to sop up the excess cortisol floating around in the bloodstream. If you have even one stress reaction per hour—well, *you* do the math. And remember, you probably don't really have to encounter some terrible threat like a wild animal on your way to school. Your body-mind, alas, doesn't know the difference between "real" and "mental" stress. That's what keeps us so overworked. Thinking about stressful things makes us work overtime. Your mind is the gateway to stress.

Did you realize that about 70 percent of cases of insomnia are caused by stress? Body-Mind owners need their sleep to be on top of their game, so this can be a big problem. Lack of sleep can make you grouchy, not to mention pretty sad. The stress-related changes in your immune system also result in making too much of certain chemicals, called *cytokines*, that float to the brain and affect your moods. It's normal to feel pretty sad when bad things happen, but too much stress can make you depressed if you don't know how to roll with it.

Last, let's not forget the risk of addictions. We understand that stress seems to be temporarily reduced by taking an addictive substance or engaging in some stress-avoidance activity. The point here is that it's temporary. You can count on feeling a crash shortly afterward. This only increases anxiety and all those awful stress-related feelings.

We could go on and on, but we think we've made our point. We want to keep on working for you so that you'll have a happier, healthier life. Here's the bottom line: The things that stress you out in your life are not going away. You need to learn how to relate to your stress in ways that don't harm your system. Working with your mind and your mental attitude is a great place to start. Please, keep up the good work.

Yours truly,

Your Body-Mind Team

My Home Practice: Theme A

1. Practice mindful breathing for at least three breaths at a time three times per day.

2. Do a short mindful-movement practice (once a day, ideally; use the audio that should be provided by your teacher). Use the illustrations for "Sitting Postures" and "Standing Postures."

3. Continue to notice thoughts, feelings, and physical sensations as they arise throughout the day.

4. Continue practicing mindfulness in your day-to-day life, especially in the area you chose in theme B, "Mindfulness in My Life." Add the practice of kindness to yourself and others.

5. Use workbook pages "More Ways to Practice Mindfulness in Action" and "Eating Awareness Calendar" to help with mindful-walking and mindful-eating practices.

6. Note your observations and reflections in the lines below.

Observations and Reflections:

A

_____

_____

_____

_____

_____

_____

_____

_____

_____

_____

_____

_____

_____

Theme A: Tips to Take Away: More Ways to Practice Mindfulness in Action

Mindful Eating

- Break out of eating on "automatic pilot."

- Experiment with eating mindfully by paying attention to all the sensations of eating.

- Try eating a snack or a meal in silence.

- Look at the food on your plate with curiosity: notice colors, textures, shapes, aromas, and so on.

- Slow down the pace of eating.

- Before chewing, experience what the food feels like in your mouth.

- As you chew, notice all the sensations.

- Try practicing gratitude for all the people whose work made it possible for you to eat this food.

Mindful Walking

- Pay attention to all the sensations of movement as you walk.

- Notice the contact of your feet with the floor or the ground.

- Notice the sequence of each step by slowing down your walking in the following way: Lift your right foot, place the heel down, and then place the upper part of the foot down. Repeat with the other foot.

- As you move from place to place, use the transition as a time to be in your body by experiencing the sensations of walking.

- Feel the movements of your body as you walk up stairs.

- Choose a period of time to practice mindful walking. Select an area or path (even in your bedroom) where you can practice undisturbed. Begin by slowing down your pace and focusing your full attention on an aspect of walking (for example, your feet, the movement of your legs, and so on). When your mind wanders, just bring your attention back to the experience of walking.

Theme A: Eating Awareness Calendar

Practice mindful eating by choosing one experience of eating each day and trying to become aware of that experience while it is happening.

Record in detail your responses to the questions below after the period of eating.

	What was the experience? (for example, snack, meal)	Were you aware of the experience while it was happening? (yes or no)	How did your body feel during the experience? Describe the sensations in detail.	What moods, feelings, and thoughts came along with this experience?
Day 1				
Day 2				
Day 3				
Day 4				
Day 5				
Day 6				
Day 7				

A

Theme A: The Triangle of Awareness

Copy or cut out this image and place it somewhere to remind you to be mindful of bodily sensations, thoughts, and feelings as they come and go. Mentally label each one "thinking," "feeling," or "sensing" in the moment you become aware of it. Watch them as they change, with curiosity and acceptance of whatever the experience is. You don't need to REACT right away. You can RESPOND instead. You can be RIGHT HERE, RIGHT NOW. In doing this, you practice strengthening your awareness of your present experience, you gain more balance and control of your responses, and you can be kinder to yourself and to others. This is the inner edge.

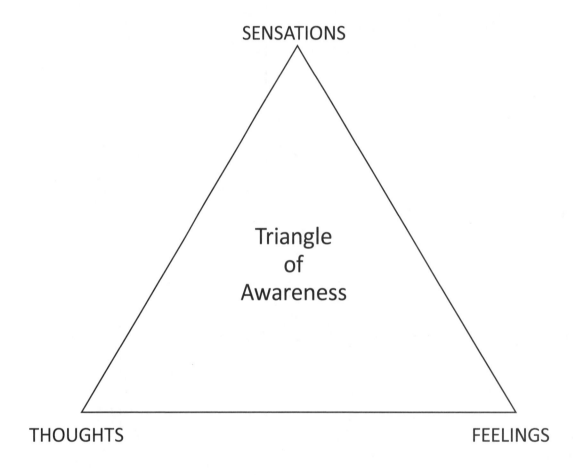

SENSATIONS

Triangle
of
Awareness

THOUGHTS

FEELINGS

A

Theme T: Ways We Practice Kindness

Thoughts

Feelings

Actions

T

Theme T: Ways We Practice Meanness or Don't Take Care of Ourselves

Thoughts

_____
_____
_____
_____
_____
_____

Feelings

_____
_____
_____
_____
_____
_____

Actions

_____
_____
_____
_____
_____

My Home Practice: Theme T

1. Practice mindful breathing for at least three breaths at a time three times per day.

2. Try to do a short loving-kindness practice (once a day, ideally; see audio downloads at www. newharbinger.com/46714). Change the language to suit yourself.

3. Begin to notice thoughts, feelings, and physical sensations as they arise throughout the day. Pay particular attention to thoughts and feelings that are related to self-criticism or criticism of others. Try offering yourself and others kindness instead.

4. Continue practicing mindfulness in your day-to-day life, especially in your practice area. Note your observations and reflections in the lines below.

Observations and Reflections:

_____

_____

_____

_____

_____

_____

_____

_____

_____

_____

_____

_____

_____

_____

T

Theme T: Self-Compassion Practice

Take a few breaths before beginning, then use this script as a guide for practice.

I've learned that everyone has thoughts, feelings, and circumstances that make them happy sometimes and upset at other times.

These are all part of the experience of living a fully human life.

I can be mindful of the comings and goings of these emotional visitors, just observing their presence in my body and mind right now.

Even if now things are difficult or if I can't understand my feelings, I can stop and remember a few things:

I'm not the only person who feels these things.

Other people feel them too.

I can step back and notice what's happening in my body,

I can feel the wave of feelings that makes me want to escape or get even…without doing anything to act on it right away.

And I can say to myself:

You are not alone.

Everyone feels this way sometimes.

May I be a little calmer right now.

May I be a little bit kinder to myself right now.

T

Note your feelings and observations in the lines below.

Observations and Reflections:

_____

_____

_____

_____

_____

_____

_____

_____

_____

_____

_____

_____

_____

_____

_____

_____

_____

_____

_____

T

Theme T: Tips to Take Away: Dial Up the Gratitude

Positive emotions provide many benefits to physical, intellectual, emotional, and social well-being. In particular, gratitude can be an effective antidote to anger, hostility, and irritation, which are bad for your health. We are used to thinking of gratitude as a feeling that comes and goes. But gratitude is also a *practice*. Recent scientific studies show that you can cultivate positive emotions like gratitude. You might have heard that researchers who studied lottery winners found that these instant millionaires often ended up much less happy than they were before they won huge sums of money. How can you explain this? It appears that happiness doesn't come exclusively from what's outside us. It's really more a matter of what's happening inside us. Daily practice of gratitude can increase your happiness in real and long-lasting ways.

Try these techniques

1. Pay mindful attention to good things in your day, no matter how small they are.

2. Keep a daily log of things that you are grateful for. Make this a regular routine by adding to the list each night before you go to bed.

3. Turn things around and practice gratitude for the things that seem less desirable. Do you hate homework? Practice being grateful that you can go to school.

4. When you're feeling low or upset, practice looking for the blessings. Stop. Tune in to your breath. Look around and find three things that you're grateful for.

5. Say thank you or write a letter of gratitude to someone who has helped you.

6. Notice the kindness of others, and say thank you often.

7. Experience the feelings of gratitude in your body around the area of your heart. Tune in to this feeling several times each day.

8. Try writing in your journal about gratitude. Here are some questions to get you started:

Select something in your life for which you are grateful. It could be a person, object, activity, memory, and so on. Write in your journal your responses to the following questions: *Why am I grateful for this? How does it enrich my life? How would I feel if I lost it? How could I show my gratitude for this?*

My Home Practice: Theme H

1. Practice mindful breathing as often as possible throughout the day.

2. Make a plan to practice a mindfulness activity of your choice (mindful breathing, body scan, loving-kindness, mindful eating, mindful walking, and so on) each day.

3. Note your observations and reflections in the lines below.

Observations and Reflections:

_____

_____

_____

_____

_____

_____

_____

_____

_____

_____

_____

_____

_____

_____

_____

_____

_____

H

Theme H: Tips to Take Away

Mindfulness Cues

You can enhance your practice of mindfulness by using cues to remind yourself to pay attention in order to be really present for your one and only life.

* Put a note on your computer screen or your mirror reminding yourself to "BREATHE."

* Drive or walk with the music turned off, for a change, to notice your surroundings.

* Take three slow, mindful breaths as you get up in the morning and before you go to sleep.

* When you talk to a friend, really listen. Gently let your own thoughts and preoccupations go, and tune in to what this person is saying.

* Download a bell sound to your computer, and set it to ring at random moments. Each time it rings, take a mindful breath.

* Choose a path or street that you walk or run down regularly. Make that your "mindful walking or running path" and practice mindful walking or running each time you go there.

* Go outside at night for three minutes and really look at the stars.

* Go outside during the day for three minutes and really look at something beautiful in nature.

* Exercise mindfully. Pay attention to the movement of your body.

* Practice taking a mindful breath before responding to an e-mail or text message.

* Center your attention by taking five mindful breaths before you start your homework.

* Continue to expand on your "Mindfulness in My Life" activity in theme B.

H